A Passion for
PASTA

AMERICAN
★COOKING★
GUILD™

Boynton Beach, Florida

Dedication

To John, pasta enthusiast, who asked wistfully when the book was completed, "Well, can't we just go on testing anyway?" And to Mom, the first of us to publish a book.

Acknowledgments

—Cover Design and Layout by Pearl & Associates, Inc.

—Cover Photo by Burwell and Burwell

—Edited by Marian Levine

—Illustrations by Jim Haynes

More...Quick Recipes for Creative Cooking!

The American Cooking Guild's *Collector's Series* includes over 30 popular cooking topics such as Barbeque, Breakfast & Brunches, Chicken, Cookies, Hors d' Oeuvres, Seafood, Tea, Coffee, Pasta, Pizza, Salads, Italian and many more. Each book contains more than 50 selected recipes. For a catalog of these and many other full sized cookbooks, send $1 to the address below and a coupon will be included for $1 off your first order.

Cookbooks Make Great Premiums!

The American Cooking Guild has been the premier publisher of private label and custom cookbooks since 1981. Retailers, manufacturers, and food companies have all chosen The American Cooking Guild to publish their premium and promotional cookbooks. For further information on our special markets programs please contact the address.

The American Cooking Guild

3600-K South Congress Avenue

Boynton Beach, FL 33426

Table of Contents

Pasta Salads

Pasta & Vegetables

Introduction

In recent years pasta has entered our lives in a big way. Supermarket and deli shelves bulge with every shape, size, flavor and color: bow ties, wagon wheels, twists and elbows; fat lasagna, thinner fettuccine, angel hair filaments. Pasta fresh and dried; pasta whose flavorings dye it all the wonderful colors of Joseph's coat: tomato red, beet pink, saffron yellow, spinach green, even the purple-black of squid ink. Once cooked, the variety of sauces is dizzying. You could feast on pasta for a year without repeating a dish—and never get bored.

What a contrast to the midwest of my childhood where mothers made macaroni and cheese, chicken with noodles, and of course, spaghetti and meatballs. Noodles were filling, not sophisticated; kids liked noodles, you took them to PTA suppers and church socials. *Pasta?* We didn't even know the word.

Thank heaven our horizons widened. With all its glories, pasta has come to stay. The everything food, it runs the gamut from light to rib-sticking, hot to cold, quickly-prepared to long-simmered. In one form or another pasta figures in every ethnic cuisine. We stir up pasta dishes from Europe, noodles from Asia; we improvise delights from whatever cuisine we fancy at the moment because the amiable pasta makes friends with everything.

In a time when reminders of clogged arteries and cholesterol and love handles assault us from all sides, it's comforting to know that in its unadorned state pasta is fat-free, and when properly sauced, low calorie. In our enthusiasm, we sometimes forget that a perfectly prepared pasta doesn't swim in sauce, but is lightly coated.

The jewel in pasta's crown is that pasta dishes are fun to prepare. Something about pasta welcomes sudden inspiration and flights of fancy. It is user-friendly. Pasta is no humorless tyrant that keeps you slogging in the kitchen long after your interest has flagged. Most pasta recipes are prepared quickly.

Pasta has star quality. Cooked slightly chewy and imaginatively sauced, it wins more applause per preparation minute than any other food I know.

Cooking Tips for Pasta

Unfortunately there are some among us who still think pasta is the bland but necessary underpinning for a boffo sauce. Italians would tear their hair at the thought. They coat their pasta lightly so the sauce doesn't mask its taste and texture.

To show you how important the pasta itself is to Italians, my friend Sue Low, who lives and cooks in Bologna, Italy, tells me that when Italians start cooking pasta, everything else is in readiness, including alerting the diners. The pasta emerges from the pot, meets the sauce, and is eaten practically in the next breath.

1. **Don't overcook:** Pasta should be cooked only until still slightly chewy. It should feel good against your teeth, and stand up to its sauce. Italians call this delicious state "al dente" (to the tooth). To achieve this, start testing several minutes before the suggested cooking time is up. If the center feels hard or if you see a light-colored point, let it go a little longer, but stop the cooking while the pasta still gives your teeth some pleasant texture.

2. **Amount to cook:** 4 ounces of pasta per person for a main dish serving, 2 ounces for a first course or side dish.

3. **Water:** Pasta needs to cook in a large amount of rapidly boiling water. Four quarts per pound of pasta is usual. That amount of water takes a good while to heat, so start early.

4. **Salting the water:** Add salt only after boiling has begun. Coarse salt is preferred to table salt, because it salts the water better and heightens the pasta's taste. Add a heaped tablespoon to every 4 quarts of water. If your sauce will be delicate or bland, add an extra half tablespoon salt to give the pasta a boost.

5. **Oil for sticking:** If the pasta is used immediately, sticking is no problem. If it must wait a bit, drain it and toss with a little butter or oil.

6. **If your timing is off:** Ideally, the sauce awaits the pasta, but we aren't always perfect. If your pasta is done early, lift it out of the water with tongs or a big fork and put it in a bowl. Keep the cooking water over low heat. When you are ready to serve, return the water to a quick boil, drop in the pasta for a few seconds, drain it, and there you are.

If you are entertaining and must cook the pasta ahead, remove it from the water just before it reaches the al dente stage, drain and cool. When you are ready to serve, plunge it into rapidly boiling water for 5–10 seconds just to heat it.

7. **Too much pasta:** If you cook too much pasta, freeze the excess. At serving time, plunge the still-frozen pasta into rapidly boiling water until the strands separate—a matter of seconds. Drain and serve.

8. **Advance preparation:** Most recipes in this book are quick. To take full advantage of the fact, read the recipe through and then assemble your ingredients. Chop, grate or measure. Put the prepared items in small bowls or heap them on pieces of waxed paper on a cookie sheet that moves easily from sink or chopping place to the stove.

9. **Have dinner plates hot:** For some reason, pasta cools faster than other foods. Once pasta leaves the source of heat, don't toss it any more than necessary because that aerates, and hence cools, it.

10. **Tossing pasta:** The easiest way is to use 2 forks. This keeps the strands separated and is gentle on the pasta.

11. **Serving:** If your sauce is the least bit liquid, provide diners with pasta bowls or soup bowls and a big spoon along with the requisite fork so all the sauce can be scooped up.

12. **Rinsing:** Don't rinse the cooked pasta unless you are using it for a cold pasta dish or you need to handle it right away for a casserole.

13. **Substitutions:** There is nothing magic about the pasta called for in a recipe. You can substitute freely. The lighter, more delicate sauces go best with smaller pastas and thinner strands. Meat sauces take well to sturdy pastas like rigatoni or penne or the shell shapes that trap bits of meat and sauce. Dense, creamy or spicy sauces go well with twisted, curly or grooved pastas that offer lots of indentions to hold sauce.

14. **A last note:** Pasta recipes fall in with the current trend toward eating less meat. In fact, many dishes can easily be turned into vegetarian meals by replacing the meat with firm tofu. Or, if the recipe also calls for a vegetable, the meat may be eliminated and the amount of vegetable increased accordingly.

And now, enough reading. Put on your apron and get cooking.

A Glossary of Pasta

• ROTINI •

• ELBOW MACARONI •

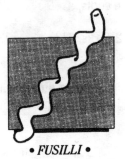

• FUSILLI •

• FARFALLE •
(Butterflies or Bow ties)

• TORTELLINI •

• FETTUCCINE •

• ROTE •
(Wheels)

• ZITI •

• RIGATONI •

• PENNE •

• SMALL SHELLS •

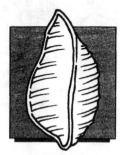

• GIANT SHELLS •

Pasta &
Cheese

Pasta with Four Cheeses

There are many variations of this luscious sauce. I like this version which uses two soft, creamy cheeses plus Gorgonzola and Parmesan to give a subtle kick. It is rich and silken and pure heaven on the tongue. Serve it in bowls so you don't lose any sauce.

1	pound spinach linguine, small bow ties or fusilli
6	Tablespoons butter
3	ounces Fontina cheese, cubed
3	ounces Gorgonzola cheese, cubed
3	ounces Bel Paese cheese, cubed
1/4	teaspoon white pepper
1 1/4	cups whipping cream
2/3	cup Parmesan cheese, grated

Cook pasta as package directs, al dente. Drain.

Meanwhile, in a heavy saucepan over low heat, melt butter or margarine. Stir in Fontina, Gorgonzola and Bel Paese cheeses, and pepper. Cook and stir over low heat until the cheeses have melted. Do not let the mixture boil. Stir in cream and Parmesan cheese. Heat through.

Gently toss the hot pasta with the hot sauce until completely coated. Serve hot.

Yield: 4 servings.

Fettuccine or Tortellini with Gorgonzola Sauce

This unctuous sauce can be made with any blue-veined cheese and any pasta that takes your fancy. The result is rich and smooth with a wonderful tang lurking beneath the creamy satin. The sauce takes a maximum of 5 minutes to prepare. You can easily double it.

- 8 ounces fettuccine or tortellini
- $1/4$ cup butter
- $1/2$ cup whipping cream
- 4 ounces crumbled Gorgonzola cheese (or Roquefort)
  salt and pepper to taste
- 1 Tablespoon vegetable oil
- $1/3$ cup freshly grated Parmesan

Cook pasta as directed, al dente, and drain.

While pasta cooks, in a large skillet melt butter. When the butter foams, add cream and bring to a boil. Add the Gorgonzola, turn the heat to low and cook 3 to 4 minutes, until the mixture starts to thicken. Taste and add pepper. (It probably won't need salt because of the cheeses.) Set sauce aside.

In the pan the pasta was cooked in, heat the oil and toss the pasta in it to warm. Pour on the Gorgonzola sauce, then add the Parmesan cheese. Toss with two forks until well coated. The pasta will continue to soak up the sauce as you toss.

Yield: 2 main course servings or 4 first course servings.

Manicotti with Olives and Three Cheeses

Oozing with creamy cheese and tangy nuggets of black olives, laced with tomato sauce; it's a favorite for buffets and one of my standbys when I entertain vegetarians.

1½ cups ripe olives
1 cup fine curd cottage cheese
1½ cups grated Romano cheese, divided
1 cup grated Muenster cheese
2 eggs, slightly beaten
½ teaspoon oregano
¼ teaspoon salt
⅛ teaspoon pepper
12 pieces manicotti
16 ounces of canned or homemade tomato sauce plus additional tomato sauce for table

Slice the olives. Set aside ½ cup.

In a large bowl mix 1 cup olives, cottage cheese, 1 cup Romano cheese, Muenster cheese, eggs, oregano, salt and pepper.

Preheat oven to 350°.

To cook the manicotti, drop four of them into rapidly boiling water and boil for only 3-4 minutes. Remove gently with a slotted spoon. Continue until all are cooked. Fill them with the cheese mixture.

Into a greased 9-inch square baking dish, pour 1 cup of the tomato sauce. Arrange the stuffed manicotti on top. Pour on another cup of the sauce. Sprinkle with reserved Romano cheese and olives. Bake at 350° for 25-30 minutes until bubbly and well heated.

Serve manicotti hot. Pass additional tomato sauce at the table.

Yield: 6 servings.

Pasta in Lemon Cream Sauce

This is utter luxury; soft, subtle, with a tang of lemon lurking under the creaminess. Served plain on a delicate pasta, it is sophisticated and elegant.

    1   pound pasta
    1¹/₃ cups heavy cream
    1   Tablespoon freshly grated lemon rind (about 2 lemons)
    ¹/₂ cup butter, cut into pieces
    2   teaspoons lemon juice
    1¹/₂ cups freshly grated Parmesan cheese
    ¹/₂ teaspoon freshly grated nutmeg
         salt and pepper to taste
         lemon wedges

Cook pasta as directed, al dente, and drain.

In a small, heavy saucepan combine cream and lemon rind. Bring to a boil and boil for 3 minutes. Reduce heat to medium low and whisk in the butter chunks. Whisk until melted. Then add lemon juice, Parmesan cheese, nutmeg, and salt and pepper to taste and continue to whisk over low heat until the cheese is melted. Toss with hot pasta. Serve immediately with lemon wedges.

Variation: For a fabulous first course, toss sauce with a pound of angel hair pasta or fettuccine, divide in eight portions on serving plates, and top each with caviar. Black caviar glistening on golden noodles looks gorgeous and tastes divine.

Yield: 4 main course servings or 8 first course servings.

East-West Fettuccine with Tofu, Broccoli, and Almonds

Chinese in flavor except for the surprising addition of cheese, which mysteriously gets lost and serves to weave the tastes together. The play of textures is marvelous: silky-soft tofu, slightly chewy noodles, crunchy broccoli and crisp almonds. If tofu skeptics are among your acquaintances, this dish will turn them into boosters.

1	pound fettuccine
1/2	cup vegetable oil
1	cup firm tofu, cut in 1/2-inch cubes
2	teaspoons minced garlic
2	teaspoons minced fresh ginger
6	cups (packed) broccoli florets
1/2	cup sherry
1/3	cup soy sauce
3	Tablespoons butter
1/2	cup Parmesan cheese, grated
1/2	cup toasted almond slices

Cook fettuccine as directed, al dente. Drain.

Measure and set out all the ingredients in small containers. You will be surprised how much quicker it is to work this way.

In a wok or skillet heat oil until smoking hot. Add tofu and stir-fry for 20 seconds. (Treat it gently so the pieces stay whole.) Add garlic, ginger and broccoli. Stir-fry 1 minute. Add sherry and soy sauce; simmer 1 minute. Turn heat to lowest setting.

Add cooked fettuccine and butter. Toss and fold, using two forks, until pasta is completely coated with sauce. Remove from heat. Sprinkle on cheese and toss quickly. Garnish with toasted almonds. Serve hot with additional Parmesan cheese if desired.

Yield: 4 servings.

Pasta &
Chicken

Chicken with Port and Sun-Dried Tomatoes on Fettuccine

This sauce is marvelous—port and cream cooked to a glossy, dark-ruby essence, with the sweet tang of sun-dried tomatoes. If you haven't used these tomatoes yet, you have a treat in store. They're imported from Italy and come packed in oil, which you can drain and use in salads or to season vegetables. Don't buy dry-pack tomatoes which have a thin, disagreeable flavor.

3   *Tablespoons + 1 teaspoon butter, divided*
3   *whole chicken breasts split, boned and skinned*
1   *cup tawny port*
1½ *cups whipping cream*
12 *ounces fettuccine*
¾   *cup sun-dried tomatoes in oil, drained, coarsely chopped*
    salt and pepper to taste

In a large skillet, melt 3 tablespoons butter. Add chicken breasts and cook over medium-high heat until browned on all sides, 7-10 minutes total. Cook them in two batches if necessary so they aren't crowded. As the breasts are cooked, lift them out to a warm plate.

Add port and cream to skillet and boil, uncovered, over high heat until the sauce reduces and large, shiny bubbles form, 10-15 minutes. Stir occasionally.

While the sauce reduces, cook pasta according to package instructions, al dente. Drain and toss with 1 teaspoon butter or margarine.

Stir tomatoes into the port wine sauce. Add chicken breasts along with any accumulated juices. Boil sauce quickly, uncovered, just until shiny bubbles form again. Remove from heat. Taste and add any needed salt and pepper.

Place hot pasta on a large platter or individual plates. Spoon on a little sauce, then chicken, then the rest of the sauce.

Yield: 6 servings.

Indonesian Soft-Fried Noodles

One of those wonderful soft-fried noodle combinations with a few unusual twists: the topping of crisp-fried onion flakes and smooth peanut sauce. You have to do a bit of chopping and cutting, but once that is done, the dish goes together in minutes.

8	ounces fine egg noodles
5	Tablespoons oil, divided
1/4	cup dried onion flakes
1	whole chicken breast, boned, skinned, and cut in 1-inch x 1/4-inch sticks
3	cloves garlic, divided
1/2	teaspoon ground coriander
1/8	teaspoon cayenne pepper
1/2	teaspoon curry powder
	salt and pepper to taste
1	medium onion, peeled and finely chopped
2	carrots, sliced paper-thin on an angle
2	leaves of Chinese cabbage or a small (2-inch) wedge of American white cabbage, shredded
2	ribs celery, sliced thin on an angle
2	ounces cooked ham cut in 1-inch x 1/4-inch sticks
1/2	cup bean sprouts
1/2	teaspoon black pepper
1/4	cup soy sauce
2	teaspoons brown sugar, packed
1	medium tomato, skinned, seeded, chopped coarsely
4	green onions, sliced into thin rounds

Peanut Sauce

3/4	cup smooth peanut butter
1	cup water
1	clove garlic, pressed
1	Tablespoon sugar
2	Tablespoons soy sauce
3-4	teaspoons fresh lemon juice (to taste)
1-2	Tablespoons canned coconut milk (optional but good)

In rapidly boiling, salted water, cook noodles for 3 minutes. Drain and set aside.

In a small skillet heat 1 tablespoon of the oil, add the dried onion flakes and stir over low heat until golden, about 2 minutes. Set aside.

In a small bowl mix chicken with 1 clove minced garlic, coriander, cayenne, curry, and salt and pepper to taste. Set aside.

In a wok or large skillet, heat 4 tablespoons oil over medium-high heat and stir-fry the onion and 2 cloves minced garlic until golden. Stir in chicken and stir-fry until it turns opaque, about 2 minutes. Add carrots, cabbage and celery. Stir-fry for 3 minutes. Add ham, noodles and bean sprouts. Toss well.

Mix in black pepper, soy sauce and brown sugar; then stir in tomatoes and green onions. Stir and toss for another minute. Turn out onto a large serving platter. Top with the crisp onion flakes. Serve immediately with Peanut Sauce.

To make Peanut Sauce: In a small pan over low heat, stir peanut butter and water until it boils and thickens. Remove from heat. Add garlic, sugar, soy sauce and 3 teaspoons of the lemon juice. The sauce should be the consistency of pancake batter or very thick cream. Thin it with water or coconut milk (available in Asian markets). Taste and add more lemon if needed.

Makes about 2 cups sauce.

Yield: 4-6 servings.

Millionaire's Chicken and Fettuccine

An elegant dish for a party or romantic little dinner. Fettuccine and chicken folded into a light, smooth coconut-curry cream, topped with melting pâté, a shower of Parmesan, and browned in the oven. Accompany with a simply dressed green salad, crisp French bread, and prepare for the applause.

Working time for this treasure is 30 minutes with two 40 minute cooking periods. You can assemble it ahead.

$^1/_2$ cup grated fresh coconut
2 $^1/_4$ cups milk
1 small onion, chopped fine
4 Tablespoons butter, divided
$1^1/_2$ teaspoons curry powder
1 Tablespoon flour
$^1/_2$ teaspoon ground ginger
1 stalk celery with leaves
$^1/_4$ cup heavy cream
1 pound fettuccine
2 whole chicken breasts, boned and skinned
8 ounces pâté de foie gras (buy at gourmet or deli counter)
$^1/_2$ cup grated Parmesan cheese

To make coconut milk, in top of double boiler over gently boiling water, cook coconut and milk uncovered for 40 minutes.

In a skillet over medium heat, sauté the onion in 2 tablespoons butter until golden. Stir in curry powder and flour and cook, stirring, for a minute until the curry powder is fragrant. Add it to the coconut milk and stir well. Add ginger and celery to coconut milk. Cover and cook over boiling water for 40 minutes. Discard celery. Add cream. Keep sauce warm (leave it on top of burner with heat off).

Preheat oven to 400°.

Break fettuccine in half and cook as package directs, al dente. Drain.

Meanwhile, in a large skillet, heat remaining butter or margarine and when very hot, sauté the chicken breasts quickly over medium heat until just done. They should be golden brown, springy to the touch. Remove immediately and cut in half-inch pieces. Stir chicken and any of its juices into 1½ cups of the curry sauce. Reserve remaining sauce.

Stir chicken-sauce mixture into the hot fettuccine, place in a shallow 2-quart baking dish. Cover with thin slices of pâté de foie gras. Pour remaining curry sauce over all. Sprinkle with Parmesan. Bake at 400° until golden (about 15-20 minutes). Serve hot.

Yield: 6 servings.

Fettuccine with Cornish Hens and Fennel

Half a Rock Cornish hen nestles on a bed of Parmesan-topped fettuccine that has soaked up all the wonderful wine-fennel-garlic cooking juices. This is the inspiration of Ellen, an artist friend who doesn't know what a recipe is, but cooks divinely. I followed her about with cups and spoons to get this gem. Very little preparation here; the time is all for oven-braising.

   2   Cornish hens
       salt and pepper to taste
   2   teaspoons fennel seeds
   3   large cloves garlic, minced or pressed
   2   Tablespoons butter or margarine
   2   cups dry white wine
   1   pound fettuccine
   1   Tablespoon flour mixed with 2 Tablespoons water
       onion salt to taste
 1/2   cup Parmesan cheese
       garnish: spiced red apples and parsley

Preheat oven to 350°.

Wash hens and dry thoroughly. Salt and pepper them inside and out.

With a large, heavy knife, chop the fennel seeds very small, or grind in a mortar or coffee mill. Mix to a paste with minced garlic and butter.

Place the hens in an ovenproof casserole that fits snugly. Spread them with the butter mixture, grind on more black pepper, pour wine around them, and cover tightly. Bake at 350° for 35 minutes. Uncover, raise the heat to 450°, and bake 15 minutes longer to brown hens lightly, basting every five minutes with the pan juices.

Meanwhile, cook pasta according to package directions, al dente, and drain.

When the hens are done, cut them in half (kitchen scissors are best here) down the breast bone and spine. Keep them warm. Bring pan juices to a boil over medium heat either in the cooking pan or a saucepan. Stir in the flour and water paste, and cook and stir until lightly thickened.

Heap the pasta on a platter. Sprinkle with onion salt and toss quickly. Ladle on 3/4 of the sauce. Sprinkle generously with Parmesan cheese. Top with the halved hens and pour over the rest of the sauce. Serve it with additional cheese if desired. Garnish with spiced apples and parsley.

Yield: 4 servings.

Tortellini with Chicken and Broccoli

Crisp-tender broccoli, chicken, plump little cheese tortellini and crunchy, buttery nuts in a satiny Roquefort sauce. Serve this to diners who know and appreciate good food.

8 ounces cheese-stuffed tortellini
3 Tablespoons butter, divided
3/4 cup walnuts in large pieces
1 whole chicken breast (1 pound), boned, skinned, cut in 1/4-inch slices
5 cups broccoli florets
1 1/2 cups chicken broth, divided
1/2 cup finely chopped onion
4 teaspoons cornstarch
3 ounces Roquefort or blue cheese, crumbled
coarsely ground black pepper to taste
1 Tablespoon white wine vinegar

Cook tortellini as package directs, al dente. Drain.

In a large skillet or wok melt 1 tablespoon of the butter over medium heat. Add walnuts and stir quickly until crisp, 1-2 minutes. Drain on paper towel.

Wipe out skillet and place over high heat. Add 1 tablespoon butter. When it stops foaming, add chicken and stir until it turns opaque, 3-4 minutes. Lower heat if necessary so butter doesn't burn. Transfer chicken to serving bowl.

Add broccoli to the hot skillet. Begin to toss. Add 1 tablespoon of chicken broth. Toss and stir. When the broth disappears, add another tablespoon. Stir-fry until broccoli is bright green and crisp-tender, 2 to 3 minutes. Add it to the chicken.

Wipe out the pan. Add the remaining tablespoon of butter and onion. Stir and cook over medium heat until onion is limp, about 4-5 minutes. Sprinkle on the cornstarch and mix well. Immediately add the remaining chicken broth (about 1 1/4 cups). Bring to a boil, stirring. Turn heat to low. Add three-fourths of the cheese. Cook and stir until smooth. Add tortellini, chicken, broccoli and pepper to taste. Fold over and over until heated through and well coated with sauce.

Stir in vinegar and pour contents of wok into a serving bowl. Sprinkle with sautéed walnuts and remaining Roquefort.

Yield: 4 servings.

Betsy's Chicken and Vegetable Stir-Fry

Betsy, a wonderful cook, stirs up this pungent mix of garlic, ginger, sesame and fiery chile-hot oil, tosses in chicken, crispy vegetables and soft noodles, and produces a tongue-tingler that will keep you reaching for just one more spoonful. You can tone down the heat, but try it her way first.

2   chicken breast halves, boned, skinned, cut in bite-size pieces
4   Tablespoons soy sauce
2   Tablespoons apricot brandy (can substitute sherry)
2   teaspoons sesame oil
1/4   teaspoon dry mustard
5   hearty grinds black pepper
12   ounces Chinese noodles, vermicelli or fine spaghetti
2   Tablespoons vegetable oil, divided
2   teaspoons Chinese hot oil (or to taste), divided
1   medium onion, sliced
1   Tablespoon fresh ginger root, minced fine
2   cloves garlic, pressed
1   large carrot, sliced in coins
1   cup broccoli florets and stems (stems peeled and sliced thinly)
1/2   cup bamboo shoots
1/2   cup sliced water chestnuts
3   ounces snowpeas, strings removed
2/3   cup canned chicken broth
2   teaspoons cornstarch mixed with 1 Tablespoon water

Put chicken in a bowl with soy sauce, apricot brandy, sesame oil, dry mustard, and black pepper. Set aside to marinate. Cut vegetables and set aside.

Cook pasta according to package instructions, al dente. Drain.

In a wok or large skillet heat 1 tablespoon vegetable oil and 1 teaspoon Chinese hot oil. Lift chicken from marinade (save the marinade) and stir-fry over medium-high heat until just cooked, 3-4 minutes. Remove it and any accumulated liquid to a bowl and set aside.

Add 1 tablespoon vegetable oil and an optional 1 teaspoon hot oil to pan. Over medium heat, stir-fry onion, ginger, and garlic for 1 minute. Add carrots and stir-fry for 2 minutes. Add broccoli, bamboo shoots and water chestnuts. Stir-fry another 1-2 minutes. Add snowpeas and stir-fry until they turn bright green.

Return chicken and juices to the pan. Stir in broth, reserved marinade and cornstarch mixture. Over medium-high heat cook and stir until the sauce thickens. Add 1 teaspoon sesame oil. Taste and correct seasoning with more soy sauce and/or Chinese hot oil. Serve immediately on a mound of hot pasta.

Note: Any combination of vegetables is delicious in this dish.

Yield: 4 servings.

Pasta &
Pork or Beef

Creamy Ham and Spinach Spaghetti

You can't taste the walnuts as such, but you will roll this sauce over your tongue trying to pinpoint the elusive flavor that haunts the creamy mix of spinach, ricotta and bits of ham.

> 1   *package (10 ounces) frozen, chopped spinach*
> 8   *ounces spaghetti*
> 1/4   *cup butter*
> 1/4   *cup walnuts, very finely chopped*
> 2/3   *cup milk*
> 2/3   *cup whipping cream*
> 1/2   *cup whole milk ricotta cheese*
> 1/4   *teaspoon oregano*
> 4   *ounces cooked ham, cut in 1/4 inch sticks*

Cook spinach as package directs and press out water to drain well.

Cook spaghetti according to package directions, al dente. Drain. Return it to the hot pan.

Cut the butter into small pieces and add. Add spinach, walnuts, milk, cream, ricotta and oregano. Cook gently over medium-low until well heated, tossing gently to mix. Stir in the ham and toss for a minute more or until ham is heated through. Serve immediately.

Yield: 4 servings.

Ziti with Ham and Romaine

As seductive a sauce as you will find. The romaine is still slightly crisp, the walnuts give a stronger crunch, and a tang of lemon gives it a snap. Serve this when you want to impress and when time is short— you should be able to have it on the table within 15 minutes.

8   ounces ziti
2   Tablespoons butter
2   Tablespoons olive oil
1   medium onion, sliced in thin rounds
$^1/_2$ cup walnuts, in big pieces
4   ounces cooked ham, cut in $^1/_4$-inch sticks
$2^1/_2$ cups romaine lettuce, cut in $^1/_4$-inch shreds
    zest of 1 lemon in julienne shreds
1   cup grated Parmesan cheese
4   teaspoons fresh lemon juice (don't use bottled)
    salt and pepper to taste

Cook ziti according to package directions, al dente. Drain.

Meanwhile, in a medium skillet heat butter and oil over moderate heat. Add onion. Sauté until soft and golden, about 2-3 minutes. Add walnuts and ham. Stir until well heated and walnuts are golden and starting to crisp, 2-3 minutes. Set aside.

Just before pasta is done, blanch the romaine and lemon peel. Either boil a small pot of water and drop in the romaine and lemon peel for 30 seconds and drain or, using the boiling pasta water, put romaine and peel in a small strainer and dip into the water for 30 seconds. Whatever method, remove the romaine the minute it turns bright green.

When the pasta is drained, reheat the onion mixture in the skillet. Turn heat to low and add the pasta and Parmesan cheese. With two forks toss and fold for a few seconds. Add romaine mixture and continue to toss and fold over low heat, until everything is well mixed and romaine is warmed. Remember, you are warming, not cooking.

Drizzle on the lemon juice, and add salt and pepper to taste. Toss gently once more. Serve immediately.

Yield: 4 servings.

Ravioli with Bacon and Tomato Cream

The addition of cream turns the forthright flavors of bacon, onions and tomato into something magical. Everything you need to make this is probably already in your refrigerator.

8 ounces cheese-filled ravioli
8 slices bacon
4 scallions, sliced thin
1/4 cup butter, cut into bits
2 cups heavy cream
1 cup freshly grated Parmesan cheese
1 cup peeled, seeded, chopped tomato
1/2 teaspoon pepper, or to taste
1/4 teaspoon nutmeg, or to taste
1/2 teaspoon salt, or to taste
   additional Parmesan cheese

Cook ravioli according to package directions, al dente. Drain.

Meanwhile, in a skillet fry bacon crisp. Drain on paper towel. Pour off all but 1 tablespoon fat from pan. Add scallions to pan and cook over moderate heat, stirring, for one minute. Lift out and drain on paper towel. When bacon is cool, crumble it.

In a large saucepan cook butter and cream over moderate heat, stirring occasionally, for 3 minutes or until slightly thickened. Stir in the Parmesan, crumbled bacon, scallions, tomato, pepper, nutmeg and salt. Simmer 1-2 minutes. Add the ravioli and heat, tossing gently, for 1 minute more.

Serve hot with additional Parmesan cheese.

Yield: 4 servings.

Linguine with Roquefort, Walnuts and Ham

Buttery-sweet Roquefort, crunchy nuts and smoky ham with herbs and olive oil tossed with hot pasta. If my husband had to choose one dish to dine on forever, it would be this. The sauce takes about 5 minutes to assemble, but it should stand for an hour, so make it the minute you enter the kitchen. Then dawdle over the rest of your preparation.

5 ounces Roquefort cheese (or any blue cheese), coarsely crumbled
8 ounces thinly sliced cooked ham, cut into strips
2 cups large walnut pieces
1 cup chopped flat-leaf Italian parsley
1 teaspoon dried rosemary or 1 Tablespoon fresh
2 cloves garlic, minced fine
1 1/2 teaspoons fresh ground black pepper
1 cup olive oil
1 pound linguine

In a large serving dish combine cheese, ham, walnuts, parsley, rosemary, garlic, pepper and olive oil. Mix well and let stand at room temperature for 1 hour to blend flavors. (You can do this up to 6 hours ahead if you like.)

Cook pasta according to package directions, al dente. Drain and while steaming hot toss with the sauce. Serve immediately.

Yield: 6 servings.

Fire and Velvet Zinger

The chile and hot pork sausage make a smashing contrast to the smooth blend of sour cream, tomatoes, onions, peppers and elbow macaroni. This recipe is streamlined. You sauté sausage and vegetables, dump in the remaining ingredients, including the macaroni, and set your timer. That's it. The macaroni cooks along with everything else, absorbing all the spicy flavor, and leaving you with exactly one pot to wash. What more could you ask?

> 1 *pound hot breakfast sausage or hot chorizo*
> 1 *onion, chopped*
> 1 *green or red bell pepper, chopped*
> 1 *can (14 ounces) tomatoes, coarsely chopped*
> 8 *ounces elbow macaroni or small bow ties*
> 1 *cup dairy sour cream*
> 1¼ *cups milk*
> 2 *Tablespoons sugar*
> 1 *teaspoon salt*
> 1 *Tablespoon chile powder*

In a large skillet brown the sausage, onion and pepper. Add tomatoes, uncooked macaroni, sour cream, milk, sugar, salt and chile powder. Cover and simmer for 20-25 minutes or until the macaroni is tender. It should still be a little saucy and soupy.

Note: You can substitute mild sausage, but try the hot sausage first. The cream transforms the fire into something quite special.

Yield: 4 servings.

Penne with Winter Vegetables

The name says winter vegetables, but this combination of slightly crisp vegetables, crusty Italian sausage, and sturdy penne is delicious all year round.

4   slices bacon, cut in small pieces
8   ounces sweet Italian sausage
3   Tablespoons olive oil
3   cloves garlic, minced
1   small onion, finely chopped ($1/4$ cup)
1   small leek, diced small ($1/2$ cup)
2   Tablespoons parsley, chopped
1   small turnip, diced ($1/3$ cup)
1   small carrot, sliced thin ($1/4$ cup)
1   teaspoon dried basil
    salt and pepper to taste
1   can (14 ounces) Italian plum tomatoes
2   Tablespoons butter
$1/2$ cup canned white or red kidney beans
2   cups shredded cabbage (about half of a small one)
8   ounces penne
$1/3$ cup grated Parmesan cheese, or more to taste

In a small skillet cook the bacon until crisp. Drain on paper towel. Place sausage in another small skillet and cover with water. Bring to a boil, pour off the water and cook slowly over medium-low heat until browned, about 15 minutes. Drain on paper towel. When cool enough to handle, cut sausage into fat $1/2$-inch slices.

Heat olive oil in a large skillet. Add garlic, onion, leek and parsley. Sauté until the onion is soft. Add turnip, carrot, basil, salt and pepper and continue to sauté for 3-4 minutes. Break tomatoes slightly with a spoon and add to pan along with butter. Bring the mixture to a slow simmer. Stir in the sausage, kidney beans and bacon. Taste and add additional salt and pepper if needed. When the sauce begins to simmer again, add the cabbage, cover, and cook gently for about 5 minutes or until the cabbage is crisply tender.

While the sauce cooks, cook the penne according to package instructions, al dente. Drain. Place penne in a shallow ovenproof dish. Pour the sauce over it. Sprinkle generously with Parmesan cheese and brown it lightly under the broiler. Serve hot.

Yield: 4 servings.

Rotini Pizzaiola

A delicious casserole of curly rotini (corkscrew shaped pasta) slathered with a nuggety tomato sauce and topped with pepperoni and gooey mozzarella. You can make it ahead and bake it later.

8 ounces rotini
4 ounces pepperoni, sliced
3/4 cup chopped onion
1 can (14 ounces) tomatoes
1 can (8 ounces) tomato sauce
1 teaspoon Worcestershire sauce
1/2 teaspoon oregano
1/4 teaspoon basil
coarsely ground black pepper to taste
2 Tablespoons butter
3 Tablespoons grated Parmesan cheese
4 ounces shredded mozzarella cheese

Cook pasta according to package instructions, al dente. Drain.

Preheat oven to 350°.

In a large, heavy-bottomed saucepan, cook pepperoni over medium heat for 3 or 4 minutes or until lightly browned. Remove to a paper towel with a slotted spoon. In the fat remaining in the pan cook onion for 2 or 3 minutes or until soft. Add tomatoes (breaking them up with your fingers or a spoon), tomato sauce, Worcestershire sauce, oregano, basil and a few grinds of pepper. Bring to a boil and simmer uncovered for about 10 minutes. Stir occasionally.

Put the butter in the hot pasta pan and swirl it until it melts. Add pasta and toss until well coated. Add Parmesan and toss again to coat. Place pasta in a 6-cup shallow casserole. Pour sauce over pasta, top with the pepperoni, then mozzarella. Bake at 350° for 25 to 30 minutes or until heated through, bubbling at the sides, and the mozzarella is melted.

Note: This recipe doubles and triples well.

Yield: 4 servings.

Steak Ribbons, Peppers and Snow Peas on Linguine

This combination is light, fresh, just right. You put down your fork from the last bite feeling all's well with the world.

    8   ounces linguine
    2   teaspoons butter
    2   Tablespoons oriental sesame oil, divided
    1   pound top sirloin or chuck blade steak cut in 2-inch
        ribbons, 1/4-inch thick
   16   large spring onions, in 1/2-inch pieces, white and green
        separated
    1   green pepper cut in narrow strips
    1   yellow or red pepper, cut in narrow strips
    4   ounces snow peas, strings removed
    2   Tablespoons soy sauce
  1/2   cup water
    1   Tablespoon cornstarch mixed with 2 Tablespoons water
        salt and pepper to taste
        red pepper flakes to taste (optional)

Cook linguine according to package instructions, al dente. Drain. Toss with butter.

While pasta cooks, in a large, heavy skillet heat 1 tablespoon of the sesame oil over medium high heat and brown the meat, lifting it out to a plate with a slotted spoon as it browns.

In the oil remaining in the skillet, sauté the white part of the spring onions and the peppers until softened (add another teaspoon of sesame oil if needed), stirring occasionally. Return the meat to the pan along with the green part of the spring onions, snow peas, 1 tablespoon sesame oil, soy sauce, and water. Scrape up the brown bits and continue cooking until heated through. Quickly stir in the cornstarch-water mixture and cook until thickened. Add pepper and salt if needed, and toss gently with the hot linguine. Sprinkle with red pepper flakes if desired.

Yield: 4 servings.

Ziti with Sausage

I always use Italian sausage for this recipe, although some versions call for Italian Luganega sausage or mild breakfast sausage. Try each and see which you prefer.

  8   ounces sweet Italian sausage, Luganega, or mild
       breakfast sausage
  1½   Tablespoons chopped onion
  1   Tablespoon olive oil
  1½   Tablespoons butter
  1   cup heavy cream
  ¼   teaspoon salt
  ⅛   teaspoon pepper
       small pinch freshly grated nutmeg
  12   ounces ziti
  ⅓   cup grated Parmesan cheese

Remove skin from sausage. In a large saucepan sauté onion with oil and butter until soft and golden. Add sausage, crumbling it with a fork and sauté, stirring occasionally, for 10 minutes. Stir in cream, salt, pepper and nutmeg. Continue cooking until the cream mixture thickens, about 5 minutes.

Cook ziti according to package directions, al dente. Drain. Transfer to a warm dish and toss with sauce. Pass the Parmesan at table.

Yield: 4-6 servings.

Turkish Ravioli

This recipe from my Turkish neighbor features chewy ravioli filled with beef and onions under garlicky yogurt drizzled with red-gold paprika butter. It's unusual, make-ahead and surprisingly quick.

2 cups yogurt
4-5 cloves garlic
   salt to taste
1 large onion, finely chopped
11 Tablespoons butter, divided
1 pound ground lamb or beef
   pepper to taste
40 wonton skins (available in Oriental foods or produce section at your grocery)
2 Tablespoons tomato paste
2 teaspoons paprika, divided
   pinch or more of cayenne pepper

In a small bowl mix yogurt, garlic and salt to taste. Set aside.

In a 10-inch frying pan over medium heat, sauté onion in 2 tablespoons of the butter until wilted. Add lamb and stir until the pink is gone. Add salt and pepper to taste. Drain in a colander. Set aside 1 cup of lamb.

Moisten edges of a wonton skin with water. Place 1 teaspoon of lamb filling in the center. Pinch together two opposite corners. Repeat with the other two corners. Securely seal the four sets of facing edges to make a neat package with star-like seams.

Slide the ravioli into a large pan of salted, simmering water and poach for 6 to 7 minutes (8 minutes if you put them in frozen). Lift out with a slotted spoon to a shallow 9 x 13-inch ovenproof casserole that can go to the table. Keep warm.

In a small pan, place the reserved lamb filling and 4 tablespoons of butter, tomato paste and 1 teaspoon paprika. Stir over medium-low heat for 10 minutes. Spoon it over and between the ravioli, distributing it evenly.

In a small pan melt 5 tablespoons butter with 1 teaspoon paprika and the cayenne. Keep warm. If the yogurt mixture is cold, warm it to room temperature and then spread it over the hot ravioli. Drizzle hot paprika butter over all. Serve hot.

Yield: 6 servings.

Advance preparation tips:

To freeze: Freeze filled, uncooked ravioli on a cookie sheet, then package in a freezer bag. Package reserved cup of lamb and freeze. Poach frozen Ravioli for 8 minutes. Defrost lamb earlier in day and add to pan when making tomato paste sauce.

To prepare early in the day: Poach 2-4 hours ahead and place ravioli in the casserole with the meat sauce. Hold at room temperature unless the kitchen is very hot. To finish, cover loosely with foil and heat in a preheated 350° oven for 20-30 minutes or until bubbling at the edges and heated through. Top with yogurt sauce and paprika butter and serve hot.

Beef in Red Wine with Fettuccine

For elegant evenings prepare this dish of rare-cooked beef strips and sautéed mushrooms nestled in a red wine sauce atop buttered ribbons of fettuccine. Add a green salad with a bit of blue cheese for a perfect meal.

4 ounces mushrooms, sliced
7 Tablespoons butter, divided
1 Tablespoon minced shallots
1 small bay leaf
1/4 teaspoon crumbled thyme
1 large clove garlic, minced
3/4 cup dry red wine
1/2 cup water
1 can (10 1/2 ounces) beef bouillon
   black pepper to taste
2 teaspoons currant jelly
2 Tablespoons flour creamed with 2 Tablespoons butter
1 pound fettuccine
1 pound sirloin beef in strips 1/4" wide x 2" long
2 Tablespoons flour, to dust meat
   parsley, as garnish

In a medium skillet over medium high heat, sauté mushrooms in 1 tablespoon butter until they are browned. Set aside.

In a large skillet over medium heat sauté shallots in 1 1/2 tablespoons of butter until heated and glistening. Add bay leaf, thyme, garlic, red wine, water, bouillon and a few grinds of black pepper. Bring to a boil and cook uncovered over high heat until sauce is reduced to two cups. Stir in currant jelly until it melts. Whisk in the butter-flour paste, over medium heat until thickened. Remove bay leaf. Keep warm.

Meanwhile, cook pasta according to package directions, al dente. Drain and toss with 1 teaspoon of butter. Keep warm.

Toss meat with 2 tablespoons flour. In a large skillet over high heat, sauté the beef in 4 tablespoons of butter until browned on the outside and still pink inside. Fold the meat and mushrooms into the sauce. Bring sauce just to a boil over high heat; don't let the meat cook further. Sprinkle with parsley.

Heap noodles on a deep platter and top with the sauce.

Yield: 4 servings.

Chinese Noodles with Beef, Cucumbers and Bean Sprouts

Ground beef and crunchy vegetables nestling in soft-fried noodles, tangy with ginger, garlic and sweet-hot hoisin sauce.

8 ounces thick Chinese noodles or spaghetti
5 teaspoons soy sauce
5 teaspoons hoisin sauce
6 Tablespoons chicken stock
2 Tablespoons dry sherry
2 Tablespoons butter
3 Tablespoons vegetable oil
2 large cloves garlic, minced
1 Tablespoon ginger root, minced
1 medium onion, chopped fine
1 pound lean ground beef
8 ounces bean sprouts, about 4 cups
2 teaspoons oriental sesame oil
1 piece (5 inches) of cucumber, peeled and cut in matchsticks
3 spring onions, cut in 1-inch lengths

In a large saucepan cook noodles according to package directions, but remove them when slightly undercooked. Lift out of the water and drain. Keep the cooking water hot for later.

In a small bowl mix soy sauce, hoisin sauce, chicken stock, sherry and butter.

Heat the oil in a wok or saucepan. When hot, add garlic and ginger and stir-fry for 30 seconds. Add chopped onion and ground beef and cook at medium for 5-6 minutes, until meat loses its pink color. Stir in soy sauce mixture. Cook over low heat for 10 minutes, stirring occasionally so mixture does not stick.

Return the pot of water to a boil. Drop noodles and bean sprouts into it for 1½ minutes, then drain in a sieve. Place sesame oil in a large, warm, deep-sided dish. Add the drained noodles and sprouts and toss to coat with oil. Pour meat sauce over the noodles, top with cucumber matchsticks and spring onions. Toss and serve immediately.

Yield: 4-6 servings.

Romanof Beef Noodle Casserole

This luscious dish appeals to all ages. Soft little egg noodles in a rich mix of cream, beef and tomato. Hearty enough for the most enthusiastic appetites, yet dressy enough for a party. Make it ahead and accompany with a huge green salad and crunchy French bread.

 1 pound lean ground beef
 1 clove garlic
 1 teaspoon salt
    black pepper to taste
 1 can (15 ounces) tomato sauce
 8 ounces fine egg noodles
 $1/2$ cup cream cheese
 $2/3$ cup sour cream
 6 scallions, chopped
 $1/2$ cup grated Cheddar cheese

Preheat oven to 350°.

In a medium skillet sauté beef and garlic at medium heat until no pink remains in the meat. Break it up as it cooks. Pour off excess fat. Add salt, pepper and tomato sauce. Simmer uncovered for 15 minutes.

Meanwhile, cook noodles as package directs. Do not overcook. Drain.

In a small bowl blend cream cheese, sour cream and scallions.

In a greased 2-quart casserole place one third of the noodles, top with one third of the cream cheese mixture, then one third of the meat sauce. Repeat two more times, using all ingredients. Top with Cheddar cheese. (At this point you can refrigerate or freeze the casserole. Thaw before baking.)

Bake at 350° for 30 minutes or until hot and bubbly.

Note: This is a good casserole for big parties. It doubles beautifully.

Yield: 8 servings.

Pasta & Seafood

Scallops with Snow Peas and Fettuccine

A show stopper. Scallops, tomatoes and snow peas in a creamy sauce laced with garlic and cheese.

    2   cups chicken broth
    1/2 cup white wine
    7   Tablespoons butter, divided
    16 cherry tomatoes (prick with fork to prevent bursting)
    1/2 teaspoon salt
    6   ounces snow peas
    1   pound fettuccine
    3   Tablespoons flour
        freshly ground pepper to taste (optional)
    1/2 cup heavy cream
    1/8 teaspoon freshly grated nutmeg
    1   pound bay scallops
    2   cloves garlic, minced fine
    1/2 cup parsley leaves, packed measure, minced fine
    1/4 cup grated Parmesan cheese

In a small pot, boil broth and wine uncovered over medium high heat for 5 minutes. Set aside.

In a large skillet, melt 4 tablespoons of the butter. Add tomatoes and salt. Cover and cook over low heat for 15 minutes. Set aside. In a medium pot, cook snow peas in boiling water for 2 minutes or just until they turn bright green. Drain and add to tomatoes. Mix to coat with butter. Set aside.

Cook pasta according to package instructions, al dente.

In a medium saucepan melt 3 tablespoons of the butter over medium heat. Add flour and cook, stirring, for 1 minute. Add hot broth-wine mixture all at once, stirring hard. Bring to a boil and cook until thick and smooth. Taste and add pepper and salt if desired (it may need pepper but probably won't need salt). Simmer for 5 minutes over low heat, stirring occasionally. Add cream and nutmeg. Keep warm.

When pasta is almost done, bring the sauce to a boil over high heat. Turn heat low and add the scallops. Cook over medium only until the scallops have turned opaque, 2 to 3 minutes.

Mix the garlic and parsley and set aside. Reheat the tomatoes and snow peas, then lift them out onto a plate and mix the hot pasta into the butter left in the skillet. When well coated, pour scallop sauce over the pasta and mix again, gently. Add the cheese and half the parsley-garlic mixture, toss again and place in a deep serving platter.

Scatter the tomatoes and snow peas on top, sprinkle on the rest of the parsley-garlic mixture and serve immediately.

Note: If you use sea scallops, which are larger, halve them horizontally.

Yield: 8 servings.

Szechuan Shrimp and Broccoli on Vermicelli

Fresh and peppery and a change from the usual. You can cut down on the hot pepper and still have a wonderful dish. The pink and green of the shrimp and broccoli look lovely on the pale pasta.

1	pound vermicelli
10	ounces broccoli, leaves and stalks trimmed
1/4	cup vegetable oil
8	spring onions, green and white parts chopped separately
2	garlic cloves, minced
1 1/2	Tablespoons minced fresh ginger root
1	pound shrimp, shelled, deveined
1	teaspoon crushed dried hot red peppers
2	Tablespoons chili sauce
1	teaspoon chili powder
2	Tablespoons sesame oil
2	Tablespoons dry sherry
2	Tablespoons water

Cook vermicelli according to package directions, al dente. Drain.

Cut broccoli into small florets. Trim stems and cut into 1/2-inch pieces. Cook broccoli uncovered in boiling water for 1 minute. Rinse under cold water. Drain.

In wok or large skillet heat oil over medium heat until hot but not smoking. Add chopped white part of spring onions. Cook 1 minute. Stir in garlic and ginger. Cook until golden over medium-low heat, about 3 minutes. Raise heat to medium-high and add shrimp and hot peppers. Cook and toss until shrimp turn pink, 3 to 4 minutes.

In a small bowl mix chili sauce, chili powder, sesame oil, sherry and water. Stir into the shrimp mixture. Cook and stir 1 minute. Add broccoli. Continue to cook and stir until heated through. Add the chopped green part of the spring onions. Serve hot over vermicelli.

Yield: 4 servings.

Linguine with Scallops, Bacon and Cream

Scallops, lovely as they are, can be a bit bland. In this sauce bacon sets off their delicate taste.

$^1/_4$-$^1/_2$ *pound thick-cut bacon, diced finely*
  8 *ounces linguine*
  1 *pound scallops*
$^1/_4$ *teaspoon minced garlic*
$^1/_2$ *teaspoon cayenne, or to taste*
$^1/_2$ *teaspoon black pepper*
$^1/_2$ *teaspoon salt*
$^1/_2$ *teaspoon tarragon*
$^1/_2$ *teaspoon lemon juice*
$^1/_2$-1 *cup light cream*

In a large skillet, fry bacon. Drain on paper towels. Pour off two thirds of the fat.

Cook pasta according to package directions, al dente. Drain.

Meanwhile, in the reserved bacon fat, sauté scallops with garlic, cayenne, black pepper, salt and tarragon at medium heat for 3 minutes. Add lemon juice and $^1/_2$ cup or more cream, to make sauce the consistency you like. Continue to cook and stir for a minute or so until well heated.

Add drained, hot pasta and toss and mix over heat until pasta is well coated and has absorbed some of the sauce. Sprinkle with the chopped, cooked bacon. Serve hot.

Note: This is also delicious using shrimp instead of scallops.

Yield: 4 main course servings, 8 first course servings.

Cheese Ravioli with Crab and Garlic

Even non-garlic lovers will lick their lips over this one. Delicate crab atop fat cheese ravioli, bathed in a silken, garlic-perfumed white sauce. When crab is too expensive, use imitation crab. It works beautifully here, and at a fifth the price. So don't let your budget keep you from trying this little jewel.

4	dozen cheese ravioli
6	cloves garlic, chopped
2	Tablespoons olive oil
4	Tablespoons butter, divided
3	Tablespoons flour
2	cups milk
$1/2$	teaspoon salt
$1/4$	teaspoon pepper
1	pound crab (preferably backfin) or imitation crab
1	cup freshly grated Parmesan cheese

Cook ravioli according to package directions, al dente. Drain.

In a small skillet, sauté garlic in oil over medium heat until it is pale gold, about 1-2 minutes, being careful not to burn it. Set aside.

In a medium saucepan, melt 3 tablespoons of the butter over low heat, stir in flour, then gradually the milk. Cook and stir over low heat until smooth and thick. Add salt, pepper and sautéed garlic along with the garlic-flavored oil from the skillet.

In a small pan or skillet heat 1 tablespoon of butter. Add the crab and toss over low heat just until warmed. Remove from heat.

Divide hot, drained ravioli among 6 plates. Top each first with warm crab, then sauce. Sprinkle with Parmesan cheese and serve immediately.

Yield: 6 servings.

Ellen's Saffron Seafood

Using prepared foods to speed the preparation can be a bad compromise, but not here. My friend Ellen, a certified kitchen wizard, makes this in about 5 minutes. She bathes scallops in a basic herb soup mix glorified with the sunny Provençal flavors of saffron, anise and garlic. Serve this mouthwatering dish and come away with raves.

    1   pound any pasta
    1/4 cup butter
    2   generous teaspoons minced garlic
    8   ounces raw scallops, quartered if large
    8   ounces raw shrimp, shelled, deveined, cut in 1-inch
        pieces
    1/8 teaspoon saffron threads (not powdered)
    1/4 teaspoon fennel seeds, chopped with a knife
    5-6 grinds freshly ground black pepper
    1   package (2.5 ounces) Knorr Fine Herb Dry Soup Mix® or
        Knorr Leek Soup Mix®
    1   cup water
    1/2 cup bottled clam broth

Cook the pasta according to package directions, al dente. Drain.

In a 12-inch skillet, melt butter over low heat. When it is hot, add the garlic and stir it around for about 2 minutes. Add the seafood and continue stirring. Add saffron and fennel. Keep stirring. Grind in pepper. Adjust the heat so the butter bubbles gently. When the seafood has cooked for about 5 minutes, stir in the packaged soup mix, water and clam broth. Raise heat slightly and cook and stir until smooth and thickened. Add more water or clam broth to make the sauce the consistency you like.

Pour over the hot pasta and toss gently with two forks.

Note: Knorr Soup Mix® is available in the soup section of most supermarkets.

Yield: 4 servings.

Vermicelli with White Clam Sauce

Don't dismiss this Italian classic as ordinary. I don't know of a more seductive, wickedly luscious sauce.

> 1 *pound vermicelli*
> $^1/_2$ *cup olive oil*
> 1 *garlic clove, halved*
> $^1/_2$ *cup bottled clam juice*
> $^1/_4$ *teaspoon salt*
> *6-8 grinds of black pepper*
> $^1/_2$ *teaspoon dried oregano*
> 1 *can (7$^1/_2$ ounces) minced clams with liquid*
> 2 *Tablespoons flat Italian parsley, chopped*

Cook vermicelli as directed on package, al dente. Drain.

In a 1-quart saucepan or 10-inch skillet, heat the olive oil over medium heat until it looks wavy. Add garlic halves and sauté over medium heat, turning now and then until golden. Press on garlic with a fork to urge out the last bit of flavor, then discard.

Gently slide the clam juice and liquid from canned clams into the oil, stirring. Be careful; the oil will pop and bubble up. Add salt, pepper and oregano. Simmer uncovered over medium heat for 15 minutes to reduce the sauce. Add the clams and cook, uncovered, until well warmed. Stir in parsley.

Toss hot, drained pasta with half of the sauce. Place pasta in bowls and spoon the remainder of sauce over each portion.

Yield: 4 main course servings or 8 first course servings.

Fish Fillets in French Curry Cream

What could be more elegant than fish fillets in a delicate curry sauce laced with sautéed apple and onion slices on a bed of angel hair noodles? Here is your candle-lit valentine dinner for two, or the first course for a very important dinner. It's so easy that there's no reason it shouldn't also become one of those family favorites the kids brag about to their friends.

1   *yellow delicious apple, cored, peeled and sliced*
1   *onion, sliced vertically and separated into matchsticks*
3   *Tablespoons butter, divided*
1   *Tablespoon flour*
2   *Tablespoons curry powder*
1   *cup bottled clam juice*
2   *cups whipping cream or light cream*
1   *pound angel hair pasta or thin fettuccine*
2   *pounds fish fillets (skinless is preferable)*
    salt and pepper to taste
1   *ripe tomato, peeled, seeded and cut in matchsticks*
    watercress for garnish (optional)

In a large skillet, sauté apple and onion in 2 tablespoons butter over medium heat until tender, 4-5 minutes. Dust with flour and cook, stirring gently, 1 or 2 minutes more. Add curry powder. Cook another 2 minutes. Add clam juice and cream and simmer uncovered for 15 minutes, stirring once or twice. Add salt to taste.

Cook pasta according to package directions, al dente. Drain.

Meanwhile, place fish on a baking sheet, sprinkle with salt and pepper and dot with 1 tablespoon butter. Broil 4 inches from source of heat for 8-12 minutes, depending on your broiler and the thickness of the fish.

To serve, place a mound of pasta on each plate, top with a portion of fish, sauce and 1/4 of the tomato. Garnish with watercress if desired.

Yield: 4 servings.

Shells with Shrimp in Wine and Garlic

This dish is heady with wine, tomato, garlic, tarragon and cayenne. Be sure to use plenty of cayenne in this sassy sauce—it will linger happily on the tongue.

2	Tablespoons olive oil, divided
3	spring onions, both white and green, finely chopped
1/4	cup finely chopped onion
2	cloves garlic, finely minced
1/2	cup dry white wine
1	teaspoon dried tarragon
1/2	cup bottled clam juice
2	cups canned tomatoes, crushed in food processor
1/8	teaspoon cayenne pepper, or to taste
	salt and pepper to taste
1 1/2	pounds raw shrimp, shelled and deveined
2	Tablespoons Cognac
2	Tablespoons butter creamed with 2 Tablespoons flour
12	ounces medium pasta shells
2	Tablespoons Asiago or Parmesan cheese

In a medium saucepan heat 1 tablespoon of the oil and add spring onions, onion and garlic. Cook, stirring, until wilted. Add wine and tarragon. Bring to a boil. Cook until the wine is reduced by half.

Add clam juice, tomatoes, cayenne, salt and pepper. Bring to boil and simmer uncovered for 5 minutes.

Place a sieve over a bowl, put tomato-clam sauce into it, and press with a wooden spoon to extract as much liquid as possible. Discard the solids.

In a medium skillet, heat 1 tablespoon olive oil. Add the shrimp. Toss over medium-high heat for 1 minute. Add the Cognac and cook 30 seconds. Add the tomato-clam sauce, stir and bring to a boil. Lower heat to medium. Drop butter-flour paste in little bits into the boiling sauce and cook and stir until slightly thickened, 1 or 2 minutes. Taste for seasoning. It should be spicy. Add cayenne and black pepper as needed.

Cook pasta shells as directed on package, al dente. Drain. Toss the hot pasta with the cheese. Top it with the sauce. Serve hot with additional grated Asiago or Parmesan cheese.

Yield: 4 servings.

Tuna in Pimiento-Garlic Sauce

An amalgam of tuna, pimientos, garlic and anchovies, in taste and texture very like the golden, garlicky rouille which adorns Mediterranean fish soups. It's sophisticated and delicious. Make it when you need to show off at a moment's notice. It won't let you down.

> 1 pound twisted or grooved pasta (fusilli, rotini, or penne)
> 1 jar (7 ounces) roasted red peppers
> 2 flat anchovies soaked 5 minutes in milk and dried
> 2 large cloves garlic, coarsely chopped
> 2 teaspoons dried oregano
> $^1/_4$ teaspoon salt
> $^1/_2$ teaspoon freshly ground pepper
> $^1/_4$ cup olive oil
> 1 can (7 ounces) tuna in olive oil, drained and flaked
> 1 Tablespoon drained capers

Cook pasta according to package directions, al dente. Drain.

Meanwhile, in food processor or blender jar place roasted peppers with their liquid, anchovies, garlic, oregano, salt and pepper. Process until smooth. Pour in the olive oil and process again just to blend.

Scrape sauce into a serving bowl. Add the tuna and capers and mix well. Set aside.

As soon as the pasta is drained, toss it with the tuna sauce. Serve immediately.

Yield: 4-6 servings.

Fettuccine with Fresh and Smoked Salmon

The two salmons complement each other: bland and smokey-piquant. Sliced tomatoes and a salad of delicate butter lettuce go well with this one.

12 ounces fettuccine or linguine
5 Tablespoons butter, divided
8 ounces fresh salmon, skinned, boned, cut in $^1/_2$-inch dice
3 spring onions, chopped fine
1 large tomato, peeled, seeded, coarsely chopped
$^1/_2$ cup dry white wine
$^1/_2$ cup bottled clam juice
1 cup heavy cream
1 Tablespoon dried tarragon or 3 Tablespoons fresh
4 ounces thinly sliced smoked salmon, cut into thin strips
$^1/_2$ teaspoon coarsely cracked pepper
salt to taste
2 Tablespoons chopped parsley

Cook pasta according to package directions, al dente. Drain. Turn into a well-warmed bowl and toss with 1 tablespoon of softened butter.

In a large skillet, heat the remaining 4 tablespoons of butter over medium heat. When it is very hot, add the salmon and cook and toss until the fish whitens on the outside, about 30 seconds. (It will cook again later.) Remove with a slotted spoon and set aside.

To the butter remaining in the skillet, add spring onions and tomato and sauté over medium heat for 1 to 2 minutes. Add wine and clam juice and bring to a boil. Boil over high heat until the mixture is syrupy, about 5 minutes.

Add cream and tarragon. Continue to boil the sauce until it thickens slightly, about 2 minutes. Return the fresh salmon to the pan along with any accumulated juices. Give it a quick stir. As soon as it is heated through, remove from heat and stir in the smoked salmon. Season with pepper and salt to taste. Pour over hot, buttered pasta and toss gently. Divide among 4 plates, sprinkle each serving with parsley and serve immediately.

Yield: 4 servings.

Pasta
Salads

Sue's Fusilli in Balsamic Vinaigrette

My friend Sue sets a gourmet table in Bologna, Italy, where pasta is an important part of daily life. Here is one of her cold specialties, with which she delights luncheon guests. The combination of flavors is seductive: tiny cubes of vegetables, Greek olives, sun dried tomatoes, pine nuts and a shower of Parmesan sleeked with a heavenly balsamic vinegar sauce.

1	Tablespoon Dijon mustard
2-3	cloves garlic, minced
	red pepper flakes to taste
$^1/_4$	cup balsamic vinegar
1	teaspoon sugar
	salt and freshly ground black pepper, to taste
$^3/_4$	cup olive oil, divided
1	pound fusilli
1	sweet yellow or red pepper, chopped
6	green onions, sliced thin
1-2	small zucchini, cut in small cubes
$^1/_2$	cup Greek olives (such as Kalamata), cut in small pieces
$^1/_2$	cup small artichoke hearts (not marinated), cut in bite-size pieces
$^1/_4$	cup sun-dried tomatoes in oil, drained and chopped
$^3/_4$	cup Parmesan cheese, freshly grated
1	cup chopped fresh basil leaves, or 1 Tablespoon dried basil

In a jar with a tightly fitting lid, place mustard, garlic, red pepper flakes, balsamic vinegar, sugar, salt, pepper and $^1/_2$ cup of olive oil. Cover and shake hard. Set aside.

Cook fusilli as directed on package, al dente. Drain and toss with $^1/_4$ cup olive oil. Cool to room temperature, stirring occasionally.

To the cooled pasta add yellow or red peppers, green onions, zucchini, olives, artichoke hearts, sun-dried tomatoes, Parmesan cheese and basil. Add the vinaigrette sauce and toss gently but thoroughly. Cover and let stand at room temperature for at least 2 hours.

To serve, garnish with a little more Parmesan, a handful of pine nuts, strips of sweet peppers, olives—whatever strikes your fancy.

Yield: 8 luncheon servings.

Pasta Salata

There are so many flavors and textures in this wonderful Greek combination. Crisp cucumbers, tomatoes that burst sweet and cool to the bite, salt-tanged feta, the nip of oil-cured olives and underlying it all, smooth, chewy pasta.

- 8 ounces rotini or any sturdy pasta
- 2/3 cup + 2 teaspoons olive oil, divided
- 3 Tablespoons white wine vinegar
- 1 1/2 teaspoons dried oregano
- 1 large clove garlic, minced
- 1/2 teaspoon salt
  pepper to taste
- 1 sweet onion, sliced thin
- 1 medium cucumber, peeled, seeded, and diced
- 1 green pepper, sliced in ribbons
- 4 large tomatoes, peeled, seeded, cut in coarse chunks
- 16 black oil-cured olives (such as Greek kalamata), pitted
- 6 ounces feta cheese, cut in 1-inch cubes

Cook pasta according to package directions, al dente. Be sure water is well salted. Drain, rinse with cold water. Drain again. Toss with 2 teaspoons olive oil.

In a small bowl, place vinegar and with a fork or whisk, beat in oregano, garlic, salt and pepper. Beat in 2/3 cup olive oil. Taste and add more vinegar, salt or pepper if needed.

In a large bowl, combine onion, cucumber, green pepper, tomatoes, olives, feta cheese and pasta. Pour dressing over all ingredients and toss gently until everything is well coated. If the salad stands a short while before serving, the flavor is improved. Serve at room temperature.

Yield: 4 servings.

Tortellini in a Garden with Vinaigrette

These curvy little pillows mixed with crunchy vegetables make ravishing salads. This one is bathed in a racy, mustard vinaigrette.

 1   pound tortellini, meat or cheese filled
 2   cups broccoli florets
 $1/2$ cup carrots, cut in fine matchsticks
 $1/2$ cup snow peas, halved
 $1/2$ cup green pepper, sliced in ribbons
 1   Tablespoon sliced spring onions, with tops
 6   Tablespoons olive oil
 2   Tablespoons white wine vinegar
 2   teaspoons Dijon mustard
 2   Tablespoons parsley
 $1/2$ teaspoon dried thyme
 $1/2$ teaspoon dried basil
 1   clove garlic, minced
 $1/3$ cup finely minced onion
 1   teaspoon salt
     freshly ground pepper to taste

Cook tortellini as directed on package. Drain. Rinse under cold water. Drain well. Place in a large glass or aluminum bowl. Set aside.

Steam broccoli over hot water until crisp-tender, about 3 minutes. Drain, rinse under cold water. Drain again. Steam carrots and snow peas until crisp-tender, 1-2 minutes. Add broccoli, carrots, snow peas, green pepper and spring onions to tortellini.

In a small bowl, whisk together oil, vinegar and mustard. Whisk in parsley, thyme, basil, garlic, onion, salt, and pepper to taste. Pour over salad. Toss gently to coat well. Cover and refrigerate for at least 2 hours to ripen the flavors. Remove from refrigerator 30 minutes before serving. Serve at room temperature.

Yield: 4 servings.

Chinese Noodle Salad with Chicken and Snow Peas

A gingery, garlicky, slightly sweet vinaigrette coats the noodles, chicken and peas. Make it ahead of time. You can use any poultry—chicken, turkey or duck.

2 Tablespoons white wine vinegar
2 Tablespoons dry sherry
1 teaspoon salt
1 teaspoon sugar
1/2 teaspoon freshly ground pepper
6 Tablespoons salad oil
2 Tablespoons sesame oil
1 piece (1-inch) of fresh ginger root, grated
2 cloves garlic, finely chopped
8 ounces snow peas
6 ounces very thin Chinese noodles, fine egg noodles or thin fettuccine
3 cups cooked chicken cut in shreds 2 inches by 1/2-inch
3 spring onions, cut in 1-inch lengths
12 cherry tomatoes, halved
12 small radishes

Combine vinegar, sherry, salt, sugar and pepper in screw-top jar. Shake until sugar and salt have dissolved. Add salad oil, sesame oil, ginger and garlic. Shake well.

Top and tail the snow peas. Drop them into 2-quarts of boiling salted water for 1 minute. Drain and cool under cold running water. Set aside.

Cook noodles as directed on package, al dente. (Note: if you use long noodles, break them in half before cooking.) Drain.

In a large bowl toss noodles with 1 tablespoon of the dressing until they are well coated. In another bowl mix chicken, spring onions and snow peas. Add vinaigrette, using as much as is needed to coat everything well but reserve 1-2 tablespoons. In a separate bowl, toss the tomatoes and radishes in the reserved dressing.

Spoon noodles onto each of 6 plates. Arrange chicken and snow peas on top. Garnish each with 4 tomato halves and two radishes.

Yield: 6 servings.

Red, White and Green Pasta Salad

This is a luscious combination of creamy pasta and crisp, brightly colored vegetables. It's best when the salad has ripened long enough for the ingredients to get well acquainted.

6 ounces rotini or any big, sturdy pasta
juice of half a lemon
1/4 cup tarragon vinegar
1 clove garlic, chopped
3 Tablespoons grated Parmesan cheese
1 1/2 teaspoons dried oregano
1 1/2 teaspoons dried basil
6 Tablespoons olive oil
salt and freshly ground black pepper, to taste
3 cups firmly packed broccoli florets
1 1/2 cups cauliflower florets
1/2 cup green celery, sliced
1/2 cup red onion, sliced thinly
1/4 cup green pepper, in thin shreds
1/3 cup red pepper, in thin shreds
2 Tablespoons parsley, minced
1 jar (4 ounces) whole pimientos, drained and sliced
1/2 cup sliced black olives
1/2 cup sliced green olives
1/2 package (12 ounce size) frozen peas, thawed
1 cup pecan halves

Cook pasta as directed on package, al dente. Drain.

In a small bowl whisk together lemon juice, tarragon vinegar, garlic, Parmesan cheese, oregano, basil and olive oil. Taste and add salt and plenty of freshly ground pepper.

Plunge broccoli and cauliflower in rapidly boiling water and boil gently for abut 3 minutes. Drain.

In a large bowl place pasta, celery, onion, red and green peppers, parsley, pimiento, ripe and green olives, peas, broccoli, cauliflower and pecans. Toss gently. Pour dressing over all ingredients and toss again. Let ripen for 5-6 hours. Serve at room temperature for best flavor.

Yield: 6 servings.

Pasta &
Vegetables

Eggplant Spaghetti

Slightly chewy pasta topped with melting slices of sautéed eggplant and a creamy tomato sauce rough with nuggets of vegetable.

$^1/_2$ large eggplant (1-1$^1/_4$ pounds whole), peeled, in $^1/_2$-inch slices
    salt
7-8 Tablespoons olive oil, divided
  1 cup onions, chopped fine
  2 ribs celery, chopped fine
  2 carrots, chopped fine
  2 cloves garlic, minced
  4 cups canned Italian plum tomatoes, crushed
$^1/_4$ cup coarsely chopped parsley
$^1/_2$ teaspoon oregano
    salt and pepper to taste
  8 ounces spaghetti
  1 Tablespoon butter
$^3/_4$ cup whipping cream
$^1/_4$ cup Parmesan cheese plus more for the table

Salt eggplant slices on both sides and let stand for 30 minutes.

In a large saucepan, heat 3 tablespoons of olive oil over medium heat and sauté onions, celery and carrot until soft, not brown. Add garlic, tomatoes, parsley and oregano. Bring to a boil over high heat, salt lightly and add pepper. Put heat to low and simmer gently, half covered, for 30 minutes.

Pat the eggplant dry. In a large skillet heat 2 tablespoons oil over medium-high heat. When it is hot, add as many eggplant slices as will fit. Sauté until golden brown, 2-3 minutes per side. Remove and drain on paper towel. Repeat with the remaining slices, adding more oil as needed. Lower the heat if the eggplant browns too quickly.

Cook pasta according to package instructions, al dente, and drain. Put butter in the hot pot, return spaghetti to the pot and swirl it to coat.

Add cream to the tomato-vegetable sauce. Heat briefly. Mix the spaghetti with half the sauce and divide it among four plates. Top each with 1 or 2 slices of eggplant (depending on how many slices you have). Top with the remaining sauce. Sprinkle with Parmesan and pass additional Parmesan at the table for those who want more.

Yield: 4 servings.

Meryl's Stir-Fry on Tomato-Sauced Pasta

A good-cooking friend of mine stir-fries whatever vegetables are in the fridge with onion and garlic and serves them hot and crunchy, on a tomato-sauced pasta. Prepare it this way the first time, then improvise.

  2 *large cloves garlic, chopped fine, divided*
  6 *Tablespoons olive oil, divided*
  1 *Tablespoon minced parsley*
  2 *cups canned, chopped tomatoes with their juice*
     salt and pepper to taste
 12 *ounces pasta*
 $^1/_4$ *teaspoon dried oregano or 1 teaspoon any fresh herb*
  1 *teaspoon red wine vinegar*
 $^1/_2$ *cup snow peas*
  1 *small zucchini, cut in $^1/_2$-inch slices*
 $^1/_2$ *cup fresh mushrooms, sliced (not too thinly)*
  1 *small sweet red pepper, cut in strips*
  1 *cup broccoli florets*
  1 *small onion, sliced*

In a medium saucepan, simmer half the garlic in 4 tablespoons olive oil over medium heat until it turns golden, 1-2 minutes. Add parsley and chopped tomatoes with their juice. Simmer uncovered for 10 minutes or until the oil separates from the tomatoes. Season to taste with salt and pepper. Set aside.

Cook pasta according to package directions, al dente. Drain.

Meanwhile, in a large, heavy skillet over medium heat, sauté the remaining garlic in 2 tablespoons olive oil until golden, 1-2 minutes. Stir in oregano and vinegar. Add snow peas, zucchini, mushrooms, red pepper, broccoli and onion. Toss over high heat for 4 to 6 minutes, or until vegetables are done to your taste. They should keep a crisp bite. Add salt and pepper to taste.

Toss pasta with tomato sauce. Top with vegetables. Serve hot.

Yield: 4 servings.

French Noodle Dressing For Roast Fowl

This is a delicious, elegant change from the usual dressings and stuffings. The noodles are lightly sheathed with butter and cream, speckled with pale green celery nuggets and butter-browned mushrooms.

        1   pound fine egg noodles
        6   Tablespoons melted butter or margarine
        3   stalks celery, diced
    1 ¹/₂   pounds fresh mushrooms, sliced medium thick
        1   teaspoon lemon juice
            salt and freshly ground pepper to taste
        1   cup whipping cream
        2   tablespoons chopped parsley
        5   pound roasting chicken, cooked and carved

Cook noodles as directed on package, al dente. Drain. Return them to the hot pan with 3 tablespoons of butter and swirl around to coat. Keep warm if necessary.

While the noodles boil, cook celery in boiling salted water until tender, 5-10 minutes, depending on how finely you have chopped it and how done you like it. Drain.

In a large skillet heat the remaining butter. Add mushrooms, sprinkle them with lemon juice, salt and pepper and sauté over high heat until browned and all liquid has evaporated.

Add mushrooms and celery to noodles. Over low heat, using a wooden spoon so as not to bruise the noodles, stir in the cream. Mix and stir gently until it is well warmed. Taste and adjust seasonings. Heap the dressing in the center of a large platter, sprinkle with parsley, and surround it with the carved chicken or serve the dressing separately.

Variation: Use a small turkey instead of chicken, and double the recipe.

Note: For a dramatic presentation, cut the breast meat off the uncarved, roasted chicken. With scissors, remove the breast bone so that the rib cage forms a bowl. Fill this cavity with the noodle dressing. Slice the breast meat and reform it on top of the noodles.

Yield: 8-10 servings.

Orange Pecan Noodles

An outstanding accompaniment to almost any roast meat, chicken or duck, or whole, small trout sautéed in butter.

 1 *pound wide egg noodles such as fettuccine*
 2 *cups chopped pecans*
 1/2 *cup butter or margarine*
 2 *teaspoons grated orange peel*
 1 *cup orange juice*
 3/4 *teaspoon salt*
 1/2 *teaspoon pepper*
    orange slices for garnish (optional)

Cook noodles according to package directions, al dente, in well-salted water. Drain.

Meanwhile, in a small saucepan over medium heat, sauté pecans in butter, stirring often, for about 5 minutes; add orange peel and juice. Combine pecan mixture, noodles, salt and pepper, and toss lightly. Garnish with orange slices if desired.

Yield: 8 servings.

Tagliatelle with Carrots, Lemon and Zucchini

This delicate creamy sauce takes about 5 minutes to prepare. The barely-cooked carrot and zucchini slivers are sweet and crunchy—a lovely contrast to the soft pasta bathed in lemon-scented cream. This dish stands alone as a main course or you can serve it as an accompaniment for roast chicken or any roast meat.

> 1   *pound tagliatelle, fettuccine or any flat noodle*
> 1   *cup cream*
> 1   *teaspoon grated lemon peel*
> 1   *medium zucchini, about 6 inches long, shredded*
> 2   *medium carrots, shredded*
>   *salt and freshly ground pepper to taste*
>   *grated Parmesan cheese (optional)*

Cook pasta according to package directions, al dente. Drain.

In a medium saucepan, place cream and lemon peel and bring to a boil. Add vegetables, salt, and plenty of freshly ground pepper. Mix well, and continue to boil for 1 minute. Add hot pasta and toss over heat for another minute. Serve hot.

Yield: 4 main course servings or 6-8 side dish servings.